THIS IS A CARLTON BOOK

Published in 2018 by Carlton Books Limited,
an imprint of the Carlton Publishing Group,
20 Mortimer Street, London W1T 3JW

A catalogue record for this book is available from the British Library.

ISBN: 978-1-78312-295-0
Printed in Heshan, China

10 9 8 7 6 5 4 3 2 1

Historical Consultant: Lucinda Hawksley

Executive Editors: Alexandra Koken and Stephanie Stahl
Design Manager: Emily Clarke
Design: Ceri Hurst
Production: Emma Smart

THE ILLUSTRATORS

Andrew Archer

Andrew worked as a designer for a few years only to realise 80 percent of his "design" was actually illustration, so he became an illustrator. He didn't take art at school but he did eat crayons, which quite possibly is where his off-beat colour palettes come from!

Anna Higgie

Anna is an Australian-born illustrator now living and working in Bristol, England. She spends most of her time in her Stokes Croft studio where she uses a combination of traditional and digital techniques to create her illustrations.

Jessica Singh

Jessica is from Australia and a graduate of Central Saint Martins in London. Inspired by her Indian heritage, she loves vibrant colour and traditional textile designs. When she's not drawing, Jessica loves travelling, walking in nature or collecting crystals.

Jonny Wan

Jonny was born in Sheffield but now lives and works in Manchester. Failure to grow beyond 5'7" saw his dreams of a multi-million-dollar salary playing basketball dashed so he decided to pursue the next best thing – illustration!

Kelly Thompson

After an initial career in fashion photography, Kelly began to capture her subjects as ephemeral illustrations. As a freelance artist, Kelly first works by hand, sketching up in pencil, before using Photoshop and adding colour with help from her trusty Wacom tablet.

Pietari Posti

Finnish-born illustrator Pietari moved to sunny Barcelona to set up his own studio. He is greatly inspired by nature and loves trying out new illustration techniques. His bold shapes and expressive style have attracted a diverse range of international clients.

Sofia Bonati

Born in Argentina, Sofia now lives in the UK. She first studied geology before completing a degree in graphic design and illustration. To her soft pencil drawings, she likes to add inks, watercolour and gouache – making her female portraits elegant and refined.

Susan Burghart

Susan is an American-born illustrator based in the UK. Heavily influenced by her graphic design background, she also loves typography. She works primarily in digital and likes experimenting with collage and screen printing.

WHAT WOULD SHE DO?

REAL LIFE STORIES OF 25 [...] WORLD

CARLTON BOOKS

CONTENTS

Congratulations!

Why? Because you've been smart enough to choose a book that's bursting with awesomeness. Inside, you'll find the totally true stories of 25 women who changed the world in different ways.

Meet the **Trungs** – two Vietnamese sisters who led a rebellion against China 2,000 years ago. There's **Catherine the Great**, who was determined to rule Russia – and did. **Joan of Arc's** speciality was leading armies (and busting stereotypes). And then there's **Cleopatra** who simply oozed coolness. (Seriously, anyone who can rule a country and get away with a golden headdress the size of Egypt is a force to be reckoned with.)

Not all of the women in this book lived a gazillion years ago. Some lived much more recently. Others are still alive today. Some are famous. Some, not famous enough.

Emmeline Pankhurst changed the world for a lot of women – and men, actually – by campaigning for women's rights to vote. As for **Harriet Tubman**, she led so many people out of slavery that her achievement is truly humbling. **Rosa Parks** kickstarted events that ended segregation in the USA. **Wangari Muta Maathai** fought for democracy and the environment. Meanwhile, **Malala Yousafzai** isn't that much older than you and already she's stunned the world with her bravery. Oh, and won the Nobel Peace Prize. (FYI, she's one of three Nobel Prize winners in these pages.) And then there's **Frida Kahlo**, who was the inspiration for the entire book.

But whether a computer whizzkid, a scientist, an aviator, a nurse, a genius, an author, a leader, a painter, a lawyer, an actor, an astronaut, an environmentalist, a mountaineer, a chess player, a footballer, a political activist, an architect or a conservationist, these women all have one thing in common. They're feminists, which means they believe that men and women are equal. (Which they are. Obviously.) And they've refused to leave it up to men to make history.

You might know what you want to be when you grow up. You might not. If not, this book might give you a few ideas. But we not-so-secretly hope that it'll inspire you too.

And now for the best bit. Our 25 amazing women were and are not short on valuable experience. So although we don't know exactly what they would say, we tried to imagine what their advice might be if they were to tackle some of the issues and problems that girls deal with every day. So along with each story of these cool women you can find out how **Zaha Hadid** might deal with peer pressure, or what **Virginia Woolf** might say to anyone who feels like the odd one out.

So yes, this book's fabulous. But there's one thing that is even more fabulous.

YOU.

Now turn the page, start reading...
and then change the world.

CLEOPATRA

EGYPTIAN ICON

Cleopatra was one of history's biggest celebrities, her life a whirlwind of war, romance and tragedy. The last pharaoh of Ancient Egypt, she famously fell in love with two of the greatest Roman leaders ever. Yet she had a dark side. It wasn't a good idea to be one of Cleopatra's enemies. It's rumoured that anyone who got in her way was assassinated... (And that included family members.) What was Cleopatra *really* like?

Cleopatra was born in Ancient Egypt over two thousand years ago, the daughter of Pharaoh Ptolemy XII. Even though they lived in Egypt, Cleopatra's family was Greek, so that's the language she grew up using. However, she learned other languages too, including Egyptian. She was the first member of her family to do so.

When Pharaoh Ptolemy XII died in 51 BCE, Cleopatra and her ten-year-old brother Ptolemy XIII became joint rulers. They also married, which was the sort of thing rulers did in Ancient Egypt – even her own parents were possibly brother and sister. (Don't worry. This is completely illegal now.) Cleopatra was quite a bit older than her brother and at first she was in charge, but Ptolemy soon wanted power for himself. Eventually, he took over and Cleopatra was history… but not for long.

Cleopatra found a great ally in Roman leader Julius Caesar, who fought on her behalf and thrashed her brother Ptolemy at the Battle of the Nile. The jury's out on whether Ptolemy drowned or Cleopatra had him killed. But, either way, he was dead and Cleopatra was back in control of Egypt. She was also in love with Julius Caesar, with whom she had a son named Caesarion in 47 BCE. She went to Rome to be with Julius Caesar, but he had many enemies. When he was assassinated in 44 BCE, Cleopatra fled the country and returned to Egypt. It was now the last country in the Mediterranean not to be ruled by the Romans. Cleopatra needed to make an ally of another Roman to make sure they didn't take over. That was Marc Antony.

Antony and Cleopatra met in 41 BCE. It was a perfect match. Each needed the other's help to fight against Octavian – Julius Caesar's adopted son – who wanted to rule Rome *and* take over Egypt. However, they fell spectacularly in love too and went on to have three children together.

Cleopatra thought she was a living goddess, so she often dressed as one. She liked to wow others with grand entrances, once appearing on a golden barge with purple sails and silver oars. And she is said to have looked *fabulous*. But Cleopatra's famous beauty often outshines the fact that she was a brilliant leader. She spoke Egyptian and followed the country's customs, which boosted her popularity with her people. She was highly educated and very clever. Under her rule, Egypt's economy boomed. It also stayed independent of Rome.

However, Cleopatra's luck came to an end when Octavian's navy won at the Battle of Actium in 32 BCE. She and Antony fled to Alexandria. And two years later, Octavian took over the Egyptian capital. After a suicide pact, Antony stabbed himself. Whether Cleopatra died because of an asp's bite or from poison, nobody knows. But she remains one of the most fascinating figures in history, the subject of books, poems, movies and Shakespeare's play, *Antony and Cleopatra*.

"

I will not be triumphed over.

CLEOPATRA

"

WHAT WOULD CLEOPATRA DO...?

 The girls at school say that your clothes are all wrong. They're either too long, too smart, too blue, too baggy, too floaty, too flowery or too plain. Is there anything you can wear without them laughing at you? What would Cleopatra do?

 Easy. Cleopatra would do absolutely nothing. Nada. Zilch. She'd know that other people's opinions are worth diddly squat, especially when they're just designed to make someone feel bad. Cleopatra would carry on wearing what she loved (probably a glitzy gold headdress, so you might not want to go *quite* that far) and know that as long as she felt great, she'd look great too.

THE TRƯNG SISTERS

VIETNAMESE ICONS

Two thousand years ago, the Chinese Han dynasty dominated Vietnam for nearly 250 years. No one had been bold enough to stand up to them... until the Trưng sisters. Trưng Trắc and Trưng Nhị were so angered by the cruel behaviour of their Chinese overlords that they decided to take action. But how could two women take on a nation as large and as powerful as China? Simple. They inspired others with their acts of bravery and led a rebellion against the invaders. For a short time, they succeeded. And many believe that it's thanks to the sisters that Vietnam exists today.

NAME: *Trưng Trắc and Trưng Nhị*
BORN: (unknown) DIED: circa 43 CE NATIONALITY: Vietnamese
PROFESSION: Rebel leaders

Trưng Trắc and Trưng Nhị were born at the beginning of the first century CE. It's so long ago that their exact dates of birth are unknown. They were the daughters of General Lạc, who was as important as he sounds – a military leader and also an expert in martial arts. The girls learned how to fight and became experts too. Luckily, this was a time when it was easy for women to do many things that would later be restricted to men. For example, they could hold important jobs such as being a judge or political leader. They could inherit property or become warriors.

When she grew up, Trưng Trắc married Thi Sách, the son of a local doctor. Like Trưng Trắc, he was angry about the occupation of their country, so he decided to stand up to the Chinese. It was a brave move that ended badly. The Chinese made an example of him, to warn others against behaving in the same way. Thi Sách was executed. Trưng Trắc must have been heartbroken. But she was furious too – so furious that she decided to do something about her husband's death. She decided to fight back.

When Chinese attackers next targeted their village, Trưng Trắc and Trưng Nhị led the fight against them. They won. In 40 CE, spurred on by this victory, they formed an army, thousands strong – and many of the warriors were women.

The Trưng sisters' rebellion was hugely successful at first. Their army took over so many areas from the Chinese that they were soon in charge of Nanyue – a region that today includes parts of northern Vietnam and southern China. Trưng Trắc and Trưng Nhị declared themselves queens and repelled the Chinese for three years.

But in 43 CE, Trưng Trắc and Trưng Nhị were defeated by the Chinese in battle. Their fate is unknown. Some say they died fighting; some say that they were executed.

Their rebellion, although short-lived, is now legendary. Many Vietnamese believe that without their brave actions, their country might now be history. In Vietnam, temples, streets, schools and a district in the capital of Hanoi are named after the sisters. Vietnam is one of the few places in the world in which women played such an important role in a nation's beginnings.

WHAT WOULD THE TRƯNG SISTERS DO...?

Q *It's simply not possible to have a more annoying sister (or brother – they can be just as bad). She's always on the wind-up. Your parental unit tells you just to put up with it, but how? What would the Trưng sisters do?*

A The Trưng sisters lived nearly two thousand years ago, when they would probably have settled an argument with swords. But that's way too brutal for the twenty-first century! So they'd probably suggest that you check out one of the martial arts instead, like taekwondo. If you focus on the speed and agility needed for spinning kicks, you might feel better. And if you invite your sister to learn with you, you might even get on.

"All the male heroes bowed their heads in submission; Only the two sisters proudly stood up to avenge the country."

FIFTEENTH-CENTURY VIETNAMESE POEM

MURASAKI SHIKIBU

FIRST NOVELIST

Murasaki Shikibu was the author of the first novel *ever*, yet the chances are you've probably never heard of her. Long before Jane Austen and the Brontë sisters were even born – about eight centuries before, actually – Murasaki wrote *The Tale of Genji*. The book, which tells the story of a Japanese emperor's son, has been called a masterpiece of Japanese literature. So how was Murasaki able to write a book so many years before everyone else? And who *was* she?

NAME: *Murasaki Shikibu*

BORN: circa 973   DIED: circa 1025 (aged about 52)

NATIONALITY: Japanese

PROFESSION: Novelist

To begin with, she wasn't really called Murasaki Shikibu. This was a nickname inspired by one of the characters in her novel. Her father – Fujiwara no Tametoki – was the governor of a province and when his wife died, he looked after Murasaki and her brother and sister. At this time, couples lived apart and any children lived with their mother. So for a father to bring up his children was very unusual.

Fujiwara no Tametoki was a scholar who loved to write poetry. He schooled his children at home, secretly teaching Murasaki how to speak Chinese – something that girls were not permitted to do – as well as music, calligraphy and Japanese poetry. She was a brilliant pupil.

In tenth-century Japan, girls usually married in their early teens. But Murasaki wed her second cousin, Fujiwara no Nobutaka, much later – she may even have been in her thirties. They had one daughter called Kenshi. But tragically, two years later, Fujiwara no Nobutaka died suddenly. Murasaki was stunned and grief-stricken. Perhaps as a way of coping with her husband's death, she began to write.

It took Murasaki 12 years to write *The Tale of Genji*. The book follows the adventures of Genji, the son of an emperor. Divided into 54 books, it is made up of nearly 800 poems and features hundreds of characters.

The Tale of Genji was so popular that Murasaki was given a job at the royal court. There, she was employed as a tutor for Empress Shōshi, joining the artistic types with which the empress liked to surround herself. Controversially, Murasaki taught the empress Chinese, just as her father had taught her, even though it was *still* frowned upon for women.

While at court, Murasaki kept a diary. She recorded how courtiers dressed in the latest fashions. She also wrote that their make-up was white and their teeth were blackened. (Nice.) But these women wrote too, and their poetry and literature are still valued today.

Details of the rest of her life are sketchy. Murasaki found life at court to be silly and superficial, and she is thought to have entered a convent a few years before she died. But she isn't forgotten. A thousand years after her death, *The Tale of Genji* is still in print. So you can actually read it! But if you're going to give it a go, make sure you're sitting *really* comfortably before you start. It's a whopping 1216 pages long.

WHAT WOULD MURASAKI DO...?

Q *Noooooooo. You've just found out that you're moving house and you feel devastated. But it gets worse. You're moving to the other end of the country too, and you don't know anyone there. What would Murasaki Shikibu do?*

A Luckily, Murasaki had first-hand knowledge of this situation. She didn't just move house. She moved to the royal court, where things were massively different from the world she'd left. So she kept a diary about it. But if she were a twenty-first-century girl like you, Murasaki would blog. It would be a great way of sharing her feelings, while keeping in touch with her old friends. Try it!

No art or learning is to be pursued halfheartedly... and any art worth learning will certainly reward more or less generously the effort made to study it.

The Tale of Genji by MURASAKI SHIKIBU

JOAN OF ARC

TEENAGE LEADER

Joan of Arc believed that God wanted
her to save France from the English – so
that's what she set out to do. The only
problem was, she wasn't a soldier. She
was only a teenage girl. How could she
dream of leading an army into battle? Yet,
astonishingly, she did just that. And even
though her victories were short-lived, she
proved that it was possible for a woman
to do the seemingly impossible,
as long as she believed in herself.

NAME: *Jeanne d'Arc*
BORN: circa 1412   DIED: 30 May 1431 (aged about 19)
NATIONALITY: French
PROFESSION: Military leader

Joan of Arc (or Jeanne d'Arc in French) was born in the French village of Domrémy as a farmer's daughter. She was also a devout Roman Catholic. She grew up during a long and bitter war between the English and the French known as the Hundred Years' War. By the time she was a teenager, the English were winning and Henry VI was in charge. The new king of France – Charles VII – despaired of ever being crowned.

This was when Joan experienced her first vision. She saw a group of saints who gave her a message from God – he wanted her to banish the English from France and put Charles VII on the throne. This was a tall order. Joan was 13. She was a poor farm girl. She couldn't ride or fight. How could *she* beat the English in battle?

But her visions continued. Voices spoke to her too. And they all told her the same thing – to gather an army and fight. When she was 16, Joan decided to act. If this was God's will, then she must obey. She visited Count Baudricourt, a local captain, to ask for his help. If he could take her to see Charles VII, she could tell the king of her plans. But the count refused. So Joan went back to see him – with the message that God had predicted a French defeat near Orléans.

When the French *were* defeated in battle, the count decided to take her to see the king after all. Joan chopped her hair into a boyish style and wore men's clothes, so she would blend in with the soldiers. And off they went.

Charles VII thought the very idea of a teenage girl leading his army was ridiculous. Yet what if she *was* a messenger from God? Maybe she really could save France... While the king was making up his mind, Joan learned how to ride a horse and how to fight. Amazingly, Charles VII said *yes*. So in March 1429, Joan rode to Orléans. Bearing a flag, she led the French into battle... and to victory. Four months later, Charles VII was crowned king at last.

Joan's winning streak lasted until 1430, when she was captured by the English and put on trial. She was charged with many crimes including witchcraft, dressing in men's clothes, and lying about the voices she'd heard. She was burned at the stake on 30 May 1431, aged 19 years old. Charles VII never came to her defence.

Twenty years after her death, a retrial declared Joan of Arc innocent. And in 1920, Pope Benedict XV made her a saint. She is now a patron saint of France.

WHAT WOULD JOAN DO...?

Q *The thought of speaking in front of the class fills you with horror. The teacher says you've got to do it. But you can't. You just can't. What would Joan of Arc do?*

A Joan of Arc was just 16 when she spoke in front of entire armies. Yes, she was probably a bit nervous. But she did it. In your situation, Joan would make sure that she knew her subject matter inside out and back to front. She'd practise in front of a mirror (or an audience of old toys). She'd remember that her classmates were on her side and really wanted her to do well. Then she'd take a deep breath and go out there with confidence.

"
I AM NOT AFRAID;
I WAS BORN TO DO THIS.
"

JOAN OF ARC, 1429

ELENA PISCOPIA

SUPER STUDENT

Elena Piscopia loved to learn. She began learning when she was a young girl and for the rest of her life, she never really stopped. In her endless quest for knowledge, she studied mathematics, grammar, music, astronomy, philosophy, theology and many different languages. So how did she do it? After all, the seventeenth century was a time when hardly any men studied, let alone women. And, for women, higher education was unheard of...

NAME: *Elena Cornaro Piscopia*

BORN: **5 June 1646**   DIED: **26 July 1684** (aged 38)

NATIONALITY: **Italian**

PROFESSION: **Philosopher and academic**

Elena's family was descended from noble Romans. They were super rich, mega artistic and highly educated. They also had strong links with the Roman Catholic Church. So when Elena was old enough, her father hired the family priest to give her lessons. And she loved it! She studied philosophy, theology, mathematics, science, astronomy and grammar. She also learned to speak many languages as well as her own, including Latin, Greek, Hebrew, Spanish, French and Arabic.

That's not all. Elena was a top musician. She studied musical theory, which meant that she knew everything that there was to know about music in the seventeenth century. She learned to play musical instruments too – the harpsichord, the clavichord, the harp and the violin. Perhaps the only reason she didn't learn to play any other instruments was the fact that they hadn't been invented yet. As if this wasn't enough music, she found time to compose it too. And she sang.

Elena had already decided – at the age of eleven – that she didn't want to marry. (And she never did.) Instead, she wanted to be a nun. But her father wouldn't allow it. He had other plans for Elena – he knew how clever his daughter was and he wanted her to go to university. He persuaded her to apply to study for a PhD – the highest sort of degree – in theology from the University of Padua. They turned her down. She couldn't possibly study theology – it wasn't something that women did. So she applied to study for a PhD in philosophy instead. And this time, they accepted her.

When she was 32, Elena was ready to take the spoken exam that would decide whether she would be awarded her PhD. There was huge excitement. Everyone wanted to hear her speak. But there were so many professors, students and invited guests eager to attend that the exam couldn't be held at the university. There just wasn't enough room. So the exam was moved to Padua Cathedral. The crowds weren't disappointed. Elena's answers were said to be so brilliant that everyone was astounded by her intelligence and knowledge – examiners and onlookers alike. The University of Padua awarded Elena her PhD and she made history by becoming the first woman ever to receive one. It would, however, be three centuries before the university awarded another PhD to a woman.

After she graduated, Elena taught mathematics at the University of Padua and became a member of many academies. She spent the rest of her life caring for the poor. And learning. She never stopped learning until she died from tuberculosis at the age of 38.

WHAT WOULD ELENA DO...?

Q *Your pile of homework makes Everest look small. Where to begin? And why is everything due tomorrow? Arghhh! What would Elena Piscopia do?*

A Let's face it, Elena Piscopia was a bit of a geek. She gobbled up facts like they were sweets. But maybe just occasionally she was behind with her homework too. And that's when she would come clean to her teachers. If there were something she didn't understand, they could explain it – and maybe even give her a little extra time to finish. Then she would get stuck in because she'd know that without a magic wand, homework is never going to do itself. And you know what? It might even be easier than she thought.

> " With an education, you have everything you need to rise above all the noise and fulfill every last one of your dreams. "

MICHELLE OBAMA

27

CATHERINE THE GREAT

RUSSIAN RULER

She might have been Great, but she wasn't called Catherine. And she didn't come from Russia either. Catherine the Great was actually named Sophie and she was born in Prussia, an old kingdom that included part of modern-day Poland. A Prussian princess, her route to the Russian throne was complicated, difficult and bloody, but Catherine cleverly overcame all obstacles – including her own husband – to get there. Then, once she was Empress, she set about making sure that no one would forget her reign.

NAME: *Sophie Friederike Auguste von Anhalt-Zerbst*

BORN: 2 May 1729   DIED: 17 November 1796 (aged 67)

NATIONALITY: Prussian

PROFESSION: Empress of Russia

....

Sophie von Anhalt-Zerbst was not the boy that her parents wished for. Disappointed, they left the young princess's upbringing to a governess who taught her French, German, religion, history and music. But by the time she was 15, the highly educated Sophie had become super useful to her family. They were royal, but they were also poor. If Sophie could marry a really important royal, then her own family would be rich and famous too...

When Sophie was 15, the Russian Empress Elizabeth invited her to visit. It was 1744 and her nephew the Grand Duke Peter – who was also her heir – needed a wife. Sophie didn't like Peter much, but she did like the idea of wearing a Russian crown. And then there was also the problem of religion – Sophie was not a member of the Russian Orthodox Church, like Peter. Even though her father objected, Sophie converted to Peter's faith, changed her name to Catherine and in 1745, they were married. But it wasn't a happy marriage. It was eight years before they had a son, and even then it was rumoured that Peter wasn't the father.

When Empress Elizabeth died in 1762, her nephew became Emperor Peter III. At once, he upset Russians and his very own wife Catherine with his brand new policies and some came up with a plan to overthrow him. When Peter discovered the plan, Catherine stepped in and had her husband arrested. She forced him to sign a document of abdication and took charge of Russia as Empress Catherine II. Her husband was later killed.

The Russian throne was a tricky place to be. Catherine didn't want to be overthrown like her husband, so she first made sure that she had the support of other nobles and the military. Next on her agenda was reform. She tackled the old-fashioned legal system, changing it so that everyone received equal treatment under the law. She put the emphasis more on preventing crime rather than punishing criminals afterwards. She also made it free to go to school and wrote books that supported the education system. And because she loved the arts, she supported those too, especially theatre, opera, ballet, music and painting. Money was lavished on St Petersburg, which became known as a city of culture in Europe.

Meanwhile, the Russian Empire grew massively. But there were many revolts. The biggest was Pugachev's Rebellion of 1773-1775, which was supported by thousands of serfs (slaves) and peasants. The Russian army eventually crushed the rebellion. But it did make Catherine change her mind about equality and give nobles even more power over the poor, to keep them under control.

Some say Catherine was an enlightened leader, others that she was way too severe. But either way, she remained on the throne for 34 years until her death at the age of 67.

WHAT WOULD CATHERINE DO...?

 You've had it with the class WhatsApp group. Everyone's having a go at you and you can't even leave the group because then they'll make fun of you behind your back. What would Catherine the Great do?

 Catherine the Great wouldn't give a stuff. Seriously. People schemed behind her back her whole life and where did it get her? Onto the Russian throne, that's where. So she would leave the group. She would block the contacts. She would know that bullies do what they do to get a reaction – and if they don't get a reaction, they stop. Then she'd tell a teacher about the WhatsApp group, so the bullies think twice before doing it to anyone else.

 Be gentle, be humane, accessible, compassionate and liberal-minded... Behave so that the kind love you, the evil fear you, and all respect you.

CATHERINE THE GREAT

ADA LOVELACE

COMPUTER WHIZZKID

Ada Lovelace was an unlikely computer programmer. She was the daughter of notorious poet Lord Byron, and Ada's mother was horribly worried she would end up just like him. So she immersed Ada in maths and science instead. Unbelievably, it worked. Ada loved the subjects so much that she devoted every spare moment to their study. And when she was confronted with one of the greatest inventions of the nineteenth century, she could see its potential better than anyone else...

NAME: *Augusta Ada King-Noel, Countess of Lovelace*

BORN: **10 December 1815** DIED: **27 November 1852** (aged 36)

NATIONALITY: **British**

PROFESSION: **Mathematician and computer programmer**

Ada's parents could not have been more different from one another. Her father was the famous romantic poet Lord Byron, known for his wild ways. Her mother was Anne Isabella Byron, a talented mathematician whom Lord Byron named his "princess of parallelograms". Their brief marriage ended just weeks after Ada's birth, when Lady Byron grew increasingly worried about her husband's dramatic mood swings and bad behaviour. She left, taking Ada with her. Neither ever saw Lord Byron again.

The last thing Lady Byron wanted was for her daughter to turn out like Lord Byron. She'd dealt with one moody, passionate romantic; she didn't want another. So poetry was out. (Boo.) But maths and science were in. (Hurray!) This meant that Ada was able to study subjects that were not usually taught to girls in the 1800s. (Maths and science were thought to be far too difficult for girls. Besides, they needed to learn how to take care of a home and family.) Ada didn't find the subjects too difficult; she was enthralled. She was inventive too. Fascinated by the flight of birds, she drew up plans for a mechanical horse that would fly with wings powered by a steam engine. Ada would, of course, be riding the horse.

When she was 17, Ada met famous mathematician Charles Babbage. He had designed the difference engine – the world's first calculator – and showed her how it worked. Babbage encouraged Ada to study further. Later, when he needed someone to translate writings on his new analytical engine – the world's first computer – into English, he asked her to do it. Ada went one better. Not only did she translate the text, she added her own theories for how the analytical engine could be programmed to do much more than Babbage originally thought it could do. Her notes were three times longer than the original ideas. But when her article was published in a science journal, she used only her initials instead of her name. Science just wasn't something that women did.

It wasn't until the 1950s that Ada's identity and therefore her contribution to the future of computing was discovered. Now, she is credited with being the world's first computer programmer. When the US Department of Defense needed a name for its military computer-control system, it chose Ada in honour of her.

And every October, Ada Lovelace Day is held to celebrate the achievements of women in science, technology, engineering and maths, and to encourage more girls to get involved. After all, it would be a shame to let boys have all the fun, wouldn't it?

> "As soon as I have got flying to perfection, I have got a scheme about a steam engine."
>
> ADA LOVELACE

WHAT WOULD ADA DO...?

Q *Your parents are getting divorced and it sucks. You have so many questions that it's frying your brain. Where do you get the answers? What would Ada Lovelace do?*

A Ada Lovelace's parents separated when she was just a baby, so she wouldn't have gone through an actual divorce. But she'd know exactly what it felt like to be part of a single-parent family. She would suggest that you talk to both parents about what's going on. She might suggest you talk to friends who have lived through divorce too. Then she would reassure you that everything will be all right in the end.

FLORENCE NIGHTINGALE

NURSING TRAILBLAZER

Florence Nightingale is famously known as the Lady of the Lamp because she visited hospital wards with her lamp held high. But did you know that before Florence, nursing was a profession that the public looked down on? She changed all that, founding modern nursing, setting standards for sanitation and improving healthcare for all. There's no way of knowing how many people she helped to make – and feel – better.

NAME: *Florence Nightingale*
BORN: 12 May 1820   **DIED:** 13 August 1910 (aged 90)
NATIONALITY: British   **PROFESSION:** Nurse and statistician

Florence Nightingale (who was actually born in Florence, Italy) was the younger daughter of two rich, cultured socialites. Their Cambridge-educated father taught her and her sister Parthenope. They learned maths, philosophy, history and several languages too. (They were lucky. Girls didn't usually get such a top-class education in the early nineteenth century.) They were both a prize catch for any man in want of a wife. Except Florence believed that God wanted her to be a nurse and if she was a wife, then that's all she could be. Rich Victorian wives weren't allowed to work. So she turned two men down when they proposed.

There was another problem. In early Victorian times, nurses had a bad reputation. Most weren't properly trained and the hospitals in which they worked were filthy. Florence's parents didn't approve of her choice. But after she went to Germany to train as a nurse and returned to care for her father, he changed his mind. Florence was a natural. So she promptly got a nursing job in London.

In 1854, war broke out between Britain and the Russian Empire in the Crimea – a peninsula in the Black Sea. Across the water, injured soldiers were being cared for in terrible conditions. Nurses were urgently needed to help. There were no female nurses in the Crimea, but that didn't stop Florence. She found 38 volunteers, trained them and they set sail for the region.

When they arrived at the British hospital in Scutari (now an area of Istanbul, Turkey), Florence was horrified. The conditions were appalling. The wards were filthy and overcrowded. Rats, cockroaches and lice spread disease. Meanwhile, patients were dying from typhus, typhoid, cholera and dysentry... and so were the staff. Yet even though Florence and her nurses cleaned the hospital and washed everything in it, *still* soldiers were dying. Even more astonishingly, more were dying in hospital than on the battlefield. Why? The mystery was solved when it was discovered that the hospital was built on top of rotten old sewers, which meant that the water was infected. When the sewers were cleaned, survival rates leapt up. Florence's efforts had brought positive results at last.

After the Crimean War, Florence was famous. Queen Victoria thanked her by giving her a brooch and a large sum of money. She also asked Florence to improve conditions in other army hospitals. Florence looked at the statistics and worked out that the deaths were caused by dirty conditions, poor food and disease. So she did what she could to fix that. Then she used Queen Victoria's money to fund St Thomas' Hospital in London and to start a school for nurses. She went on to write about caring for patients, introducing the idea that wards should be bright and clean, with different wards for different illnesses. Her recommendations are still followed today.

In 1907, Florence was awarded the Order of Merit, the first woman ever to receive the honour. And every year on her birthday, nurses celebrate International Nurses' Day to remember the woman who boosted their profession so much.

> " I think one's feelings waste themselves in words; they ought all to be distilled into actions which bring results.

FLORENCE NIGHTINGALE "

WHAT WOULD FLORENCE DO....?

 Q *Someone you love is ill. You're really worried. When are they going to get better? You hate to see them so poorly. And besides, you miss spending time with them. What would Florence Nightingale do?*

 A This is a no-brainer. Florence Nightingale was probably the world's most famous nurse. So she would try to make them feel better. If she had to go to school like you, this might mean visiting them after school or at the weekend. Perhaps she would take along board games or books. Maybe she'd just chat. But she'd do what she could to make her patient feel happy, and hopefully healthy soon.

HARRIET TUBMAN

FABULOUS FEMINIST

Two centuries ago, Harriet Tubman was born into slavery. Her life was tougher than you can ever imagine. But she was *determined* to escape. Once she did, she risked everything to help others escape too. During her long life, she campaigned for the abolition of slavery, for black people's and women's civil rights and for their right to vote. She's now an American icon.

NAME: *Araminta Ross*

BORN: circa 1820   DIED: 10 March 1913 (aged about 93)

NATIONALITY: American

PROFESSION: Civil rights activist and civil war nurse

No one is exactly sure of Harriet Tubman's date of birth, because at the beginning of the nineteenth century, slave owners didn't keep records – and her parents were both slaves. Born Araminta Ross (to find out why she changed her name, read on…), she lived on a large plantation in Maryland with her parents and eight brothers and sisters. When she was very young, she worked as a nursemaid and on the plantation itself. It was tough, physical work and like other slaves, she was poorly fed and beaten often.

In her early teens, she was protecting another slave from harm when an iron weight hit her instead, causing a terrible head injury. She later said that the reason she hadn't died was her thick, thick hair, which "stuck out like a bushel basket". Even so, it took her months to recover. When she was older, she had brain surgery without anaesthetic – how unbelievably hardcore is *that*? – but she suffered from seizures, headaches and buzzing in her ears for the rest of her life.

In 1844, Araminta married John Tubman, but life didn't get any easier. She still worked hard in the blistering heat and she was still beaten often. Even worse, there was a real danger that she might be sold to another plantation. So, she decided to take action. She wouldn't wait to be sold; she would run away, to the northern states of the USA where slavery had been abolished. She changed her name to Harriet (in honour of her mother) so it would be trickier to find her. And on 17 September 1849, in the dark of night, she set off…

Harriet's guide was the North Star, which showed her the way to freedom. But she received help on the way north. People who were eager to help runaway slaves used signals – carpets or lights hung outside their homes – to show that it was safe to stop there, and came to be called "conductors". This route became known as the Underground Railroad. When at last she reached Philadelphia, Harriet was overjoyed. She was FREE! But instead of starting a new life, Harriet went back and rescued her family. Then she went back again and again to guide more slaves along the Underground Railroad to freedom. But then the law changed and slaves had to travel to Canada to reach safety. This didn't stop Harriet, who soon became an Underground Railroad conductor herself. In total, she helped around 300 people escape the horror of slavery. The song *Swing Low, Sweet Chariot* was used as a secret signal to a slave that they were about to be smuggled onwards on their journey to freedom. She was never caught and neither was a single one of the slaves she helped to escape.

And still, that's not all. In the American Civil War (1861–1865), Harriet Tubman nursed injured soldiers, while also working as a spy *and* helping to rescue a further 750 slaves. She went on to campaign for black people's civil rights. If ever you feel lost or helpless, ask yourself this: what would Harriet Tubman do?

"Every great dream begins with a dreamer. Always remember, you have within you the strength, the patience, and the passion to reach for the stars to change the world."

HARRIET TUBMAN

WHAT WOULD HARRIET DO...?

Q *Someone else is being bullied at school. You'd like to help, but you're scared that if you do, the bullies will target you too. What would Harriet Tubman do?*

A Harriet Tubman knew what it was like to be treated badly. She was a slave who escaped slavery. But she didn't stop there. She helped others to escape too. Lots of them. So she would want you to help if you see someone being bullied. Don't watch, because bullies love that. If it's safe to do so, then stand up for the person being bullied. Otherwise, tell a grown-up what's happening. Then offer your support to the person being bullied. You'll make them feel a whole lot better.

EMMELINE PANKHURST

SUPER SUFFRAGETTE

OK. Let's get one thing straight. Suffrage isn't about suffering. It's about the right to vote in political elections. And that's exactly what Emmeline Pankhurst wanted: the right to vote in the UK. Unbelievably, when she was born, women *couldn't* vote. Not a single one. And not a lot of men could, either. Emmeline Pankhurst wanted to change all that. The problem was, not everyone agreed with her...

NAME: *Emmeline Pankhurst*
BORN: 15 July 1858   DIED: 14 June 1928 (aged 69)
NATIONALITY: British
PROFESSION: Suffragette

Emmeline Goulden's family wasn't known for keeping quiet, so it's not surprising that she was so good at standing up for her beliefs. Her father was a town councillor and an actor. Her grandparents were involved in political unrest. Meanwhile, her mother read the *Women's Suffrage Journal* and when Emmeline was just 14, she took her along to hear the editor speak about suffrage. It was the first of many such meetings. After Emmeline finished her education in Paris she returned to the UK and met a lawyer called Richard Pankhurst, who was a huge supporter of women's suffrage. They were soon married, and went on to have five children.

Together, they worked hard to promote women's rights via the Women's Franchise League, but supporters could not agree on exactly which women should get the vote (the Pankhursts thought that they all should, while some thought it should just be single women and widows), so the league disbanded.

When Emmeline was just 40, her husband died. Grief-stricken, she now had a family to support on her own, but she didn't forget about women's suffrage. She formed the Women's Social and Political Union (WSPU) in 1903. Its purpose was to win the vote for women.

People had been campaigning for women's suffrage for years and nothing had changed. So the WSPU decided to do something different. They decided to stop being polite about it; they decided to **MAKE SOME NOISE**. Perhaps then people would start to take notice. So they shouted at public meetings. They went on protests and demonstrations. And, controversially, they broke the law. They chained themselves to railings, spat at police, attacked works of art, smashed windows, bombed a railway station and set fire to postboxes and buildings.

The WSPU's action worked. Now everyone knew about the protesters – they were even given a new name: suffragettes, due to their confrontational tactics (as opposed to suffragists). The downside was that the suffragettes' actions also landed them in prison, or worse.

Then the First World War happened Emmeline suspended all action and helped the war effort. And a month after the war ended, parliament finally gave the vote to some women – those over 30 with property. Why then? Maybe they realised that the suffragettes were right. Ten years later, an act of parliament gave all men *and* women over 21 the vote, at last.

WHAT WOULD EMMELINE DO...?

Q *You feel like all the other girls in your class are smarter, funnier, sportier and cooler than you. Sometimes, it feels as if you're surrounded by overachievers. You're just not good enough... What would Emmeline Pankhurst do?*

A Emmeline Pankhurst would ask you to look in the mirror and see the amazing girl there. She'd remind you that everyone is important and everyone's opinions count. That's why she fought for the rights of every single woman to vote for her future. Then she'd point out what you *are* totally fabulous at, even if it's something a little out of the ordinary. After all, there's something cool in everyone.

MARIE CURIE

FAB PHYSICIST

Marie Curie was a Nobel Prize-winning physicist and chemist. But her science stardom didn't come easily. First she had to fight to be able to study science at all. Then she spent years carrying out research in an old shed. But her hard work paid off. And thank goodness it did.

NAME: *Maria Skłodowska Curie*

BORN: 7 November 1867   DIED: 4 July 1934 (aged 66)

NATIONALITY: Polish-French

PROFESSION: Scientist

Marie Curie started life as Maria Skłodowska in Warsaw, Poland. In the early twentieth century, life wasn't much fun in Poland for those who didn't agree with Russian rule. Science in schools was banned. But Maria's parents were teachers. And not to be beaten, her father simply brought his lab home from school and taught his children there instead.

Maria was a top student, but getting a higher education was a problem. Only men were allowed to go to university in Poland. So she attended an illegal school named "the Floating University", which changed its location regularly to avoid Russian officials, while saving up to go to the Sorbonne – a famous university in Paris. It took until she was 24 to get there. When she reached France at last, Maria – who then changed her name to Marie – dived straight into her studies of physics and mathematical sciences.

It was at the Sorbonne that Marie met Pierre Curie, a physics professor. They married in 1895 and went on to become one of the greatest double acts in the history of science. Intrigued by Henri Becquerel's discovery of radioactivity, the Curies carried on the research. They actually invented the term "radioactivity". And after many years of hard work, they isolated the radioactive elements polonium and radium. Their discoveries would make an enormous contribution to the treatment of cancer.

In 1906, Pierre Curie was tragically killed when crossing the road. Shattered by the loss, Marie succeeded Pierre as Professor of General Physics and became the first female professor at the Sorbonne. In 1914, she was made Director of the Curie Laboratory at the Radium Institute of the University of Paris. Whenever she could, she encouraged the use of radium to help patients. During the First World War, she organised a fleet of mobile X-ray units to diagnose soldiers' injuries nearer the battlefield. She trained others to use the X-ray machines and even drove the trucks – known as "petites Curies", which means "little Curies", and thought to have helped over 1 million soldiers during the war – herself. She died in 1934 at the age of 66, as a result of her long-term exposure to radiation.

Marie and Pierre Curie and Henri Becquerel were jointly awarded the Nobel Prize for Physics in 1903. She was the first woman ever to be awarded a Nobel Prize. In 1911, she was awarded the Nobel Prize for Chemistry too. She is the only woman to have won two Nobel Prizes. (So far.) And she is also the only person to have won a Nobel Prize in two different sciences. (So far.) To top it off, Marie's daughter Irène Joliot-Curie won a further Nobel Prize for Chemistry in 1935, making them the only Nobel Prize-winning mother and daughter to date. So if anyone ever tells you that girls and science don't mix, show them this book. (And then whack them with it.)

> "Life is not easy for any of us. But what of that? We must have perseverance and above all confidence in ourselves. We must believe that we are gifted for something and that this thing must be attained."

MARIE CURIE

WHAT WOULD MARIE DO...?

Q *There's going to be a test at school soon. It's a big one. You're so, so worried about failing it. What would Marie Curie do?*

A Marie Curie was a hard worker. Her big discoveries didn't happen overnight; she spent YEARS experimenting first. This means she would probably suggest that revision, revision and more revision is the way to pass your test. (Sorry.) But don't stick your nose in a book straight away. Marie was also a teacher, so she'd know that they can help calm your fears. (And if some of the facts are fuzzy, they can help with that too.)

VIRGINIA WOOLF

FREE THINKER

At the turn of the twentieth century in the UK, women's lives were pretty much mapped out for them. They married young and they raised a family. End of story. Virginia Woolf became famous for bucking the trend, becoming an author and living an entirely different sort of life. Some of her choices raised eyebrows. But Virginia didn't care. She was doing exactly what she wanted to do. And she was making a success of it.

NAME: *Adeline Virginia Stephen Woolf*

BORN: 25 January 1882   DIED: 28 March 1941 (aged 59)

NATIONALITY: British

PROFESSION: Author and journalist

Virginia Stephen was born into a family that oozed culture. Her father was an author and a history scholar, while her mother had modelled for famous painters. Both had been widowed before marrying each other and Virginia grew up with half-siblings, as well as her own sister Vanessa and two brothers, Adrian and Thoby. The boys were sent to school and then to Cambridge University, while the girls were taught at home. (Luckily, they had a huge library.) But even though she and Vanessa were taught the Classics, English literature, Latin, French and History by their parents, Virginia was still resentful. Why shouldn't girls receive the same education as boys?!

Virginia had always loved writing. (The act of writing was important too – she would often hunt for a pen that felt just right.) But she didn't start writing professionally until she was 18. Her very first article – about the Brontë sisters' home in Haworth – was published four years later and she went on to write for the *Times Literary Supplement* too. She was not permitted, as a woman, to study at King's College, but had to go to the "King's Ladies Department" in a different – and much smaller – building. There, she met people who were keen to reform women's higher education – one of the topics close to her own heart.

Throughout her life, Virginia suffered many bouts of depression. When she was just 13 her mother died, and her first nervous breakdown happened. A few years later, after her father and then her brother Thoby died, she attempted suicide and was admitted to hospital, suffering from anxiety and depression. Afterwards, Vanessa and her younger brother Adrian sold their home and the family moved to Bloomsbury, an elegant area of central London known for its museums, universities and medical institutions. Thanks to Virginia and her friends, it would soon be known for something entirely different – the Bloomsbury Group, a circle of English writers, intellectuals and artists.

Bloomsbury was home to so many clever, literary and arty people that they began to get together to discuss ideas. Many became involved with each other, including Virginia, who met her husband Leonard Woolf. She was also involved with the famous poet and garden designer Vita Sackville-West. Soon, the Bloomsbury Group had become famous for their modern ideas about literature, art, feminism and pacifism.

Meanwhile, Virginia's first novel – *The Voyage Out* – was published in 1915. Two years later, she and Leonard set up the Hogarth Press, which published most of her other works, including the novels *Mrs Dalloway* (1925) and *To the Lighthouse* (1927). Her stream-of-consciousness writing was new and poetic, and readers loved it. Her most famous non-fiction work was *A Room of One's Own* (1929). In it, she argued that in order to write, women needed to have their own space in which to work and enough money to support them while they did it, privileges that were at that time often only available to men.

Sadly, the Second World War set off Virginia's depression for a final time. In 1941, she filled her coat pockets with stones and walked into the River Ouse, where she drowned. But her writing lives on.

> " Indeed, I would venture to guess that Anon, who wrote so many poems without signing them, was often a woman. "
>
> VIRGINIA WOOLF

WHAT WOULD VIRGINIA DO...?

 Q *You're an alien. That's seriously the only explanation. Why else would you feel as if you're different from everyone else on this planet? Should you try to change? What would Virginia Woolf do?*

 A Virginia Woolf wasn't like most people, but she accepted herself just as she was. So she most certainly would not change. She would know that it's OK not to be or to feel like everyone else. Who's to say they're right and you're not anyway? She might also suggest that it's possible you're NOT the only person in the world to feel as you do and that, sooner or later, you might bump into a kindred spirit.

AMELIA EARHART

PIONEER PILOT

Amelia Earhart is best known for her fabulous flying achievements in the twentieth century. But she is also an inspiration for supporters of equal rights for women and men today. She encouraged women to consider all careers, including those traditionally thought of as being for men. And by excelling in her own career of aviation, she proved that the sky really was the limit!

NAME: *Amelia Mary Earhart*
BORN: 24 July 1897   DISAPPEARED: 2 July 1937 (aged 39)
NATIONALITY: American   PROFESSION: Aviator

Amelia Earhart didn't behave like many people thought girls should behave at the beginning of the last century. Knitting and sewing? Pah! She was a tree-climbing, sledge-riding, rat-hunting kind of a girl. Just because people told her that engineering, film directing and law weren't for girls didn't mean that she didn't think she could do them. Instead, she kept a scrapbook of women who excelled in these areas.

A pilot dived at Amelia at an airshow when she was only 10. Maybe he meant to scare her. But if so, then he did completely the opposite. He made her want to fly. Thirteen years later, she went on her first flight. Instantly, she was hooked.

On 3 January 1921, Amelia took off on her very first flying lesson. Six months later, not only was she a pilot, she'd saved enough of her wages to buy her own plane too. It was a bright-yellow biplane – she called it *The Canary*. Next, she decided to start setting aviation records, just like men. The following year, she became the first woman to fly to an altitude of 4,267 metres.

In 1928, she was asked if she would like to become the first woman to fly across the Atlantic. It was a no-brainer. Of course she would. And she did, with her crewmates Bill Stultz and Slim Gordon. They left Newfoundland on 17 June 1928 and made history 21 hours later when they landed in Wales. Now she wasn't just famous in America – where her return to New York City was celebrated with a tickertape parade – she was famous around the world!

Amelia briefly took a break from setting records to marry publisher George F Putnam. She had a very modern view of their marriage, speaking of it as a "partnership" with "dual control". She kept her own name.

From then on, records tumbled, one after another. Only one other person had flown the Atlantic solo – Charles Lindbergh. Amelia wanted to be the second person to do it – and the first woman. In 1932, she did it. In 1935, she was the first person to fly solo across the Pacific and the first to fly solo from Mexico City to Newark. She wasn't matching records set by men any more. She was setting brand new records.

And then came the Big One. Could she fly around the world? She was going to give it a good try. She and her navigator, Fred Noonan, took off from Miami, Florida on 1 June 1937. Four weeks later, their Lockheed Electra 10E landed in Papua New Guinea. On 2 July, it took off, en route for a tiny island in the middle of the Pacific. Unfortunately Amelia Earhart never made it. But the world has never forgotten that she tried.

WHAT WOULD AMELIA DO...?

Q *Even the dog has a better mobile phone than you. Well, no. Not really. But that's what it feels like. You're desperate for a new one, but guess what? The grown-up in your life says a big fat NO. What would Amelia Earhart do?*

A Amelia Earhart was desperate for something far bigger and more expensive than a mobile. She wanted an aeroplane. No way was anyone going to buy one of those for her! So she worked for a telephone company, as a lorry driver and as a photographer to pay for an aeroplane. And she would probably suggest that you do the same until you've saved up to buy a phone. Quick, volunteer for odd jobs around the house!

> "Please know I am quite aware of the hazards. I want to do it because I want to do it. Women must try to do things as men have tried. When they fail, their failure must be but a challenge to others."

EXCERPT FROM AMELIA EARHART'S
LETTER TO HER HUSBAND BEFORE HER LAST FLIGHT.

FRIDA KAHLO

REBEL ARTIST

Frida Kahlo is famous for many
things. She's famous for her artwork,
especially her stunningly surreal
self-portraits. She's famous for
being a rebel. But perhaps she is
most famous for being a feminist
icon. Frida refused to act as everyone
expected a woman to act. She did
what *she* wanted to do. And she
described her life story using art.

NAME: *Magdalena Carmen Frida Kahlo y Calderón*
BORN: 6 July 1907 DIED: 13 July 1954 (aged 47)
NATIONALITY: Mexican
PROFESSION: Artist

Born in Mexico City in the early twentieth century, Frida never expected to be an artist. She wanted to be a doctor. But when she was 18, a bus crash ended her dream – and very nearly her life. She was speared by a metal handrail and broke so many bones that despite many, many operations, she suffered terrible pain for the rest of her life.

But she didn't give up. Frida had always loved to paint and now she decorated her full-body cast with beautiful butterflies. When her parents gave her a special easel that she could use from her bed, she painted on canvas too. Many of her paintings were self-portraits that showed her pain. At long last, she began to recover and eventually to walk again.

Frida Kahlo was a Communist – she believed that land, businesses and property should be owned and shared by everyone. In 1928, she met fellow Communist Diego Rivera, a Mexican artist famous for painting murals, and asked what he thought of her work.

He saw how talented she was and encouraged Frida to paint. The next year they were married, but their relationship was stormy. They divorced in 1939, only to remarry the following year. Many of Frida's paintings show the turmoil she felt.

Frida's artwork was very distinctive. Her bright, symbolic style reflected Mexican culture. Her colours were vibrant – but they held meaning too. For example, to Frida, the colour of leaf green symbolised sadness and science. Yellow stood for madness, sickness, fear and joy.

In 1938, she travelled alone to her first solo exhibition in New York City. More exhibitions followed, and soon her work started being displayed around the world. But still she was famous only for being Diego Rivera's wife. Meanwhile, illness plagued her and her health worsened, and she died in 1954.

Frida Kahlo was not well-known until over twenty years after her death. Today, she is one of the most famous artists in the world. While her work is often described as surrealism or magical realism, she denied this. "I never painted dreams," she said. "I painted my own reality."

> " The only thing I know is that I paint because I need to, and I paint whatever passes through my head without any other consideration. "
>
> FRIDA KAHLO

WHAT WOULD FRIDA DO...?

All the girls in magazines are tall and slim, with beautiful clear skin. They don't have a pointy nose or a big bottom. You can't even bear to look in the mirror you look so totally horrible. What would Frida Kahlo do?

Frida Kahlo's eyebrows were so thick and bushy they met in the middle. She had a bit of a moustache. Did she mind? No, she did not. If anything, she bigged up these features in her self-portraits because she was proud of the way she looked. And she would tell you to be proud too. So what if you're not tall and slim? So what if you have spots? That's because you're not airbrushed like the girls in the magazines. They might appear perfect, but you're real. And, FYI, you're FABULOUS!

ROSA PARKS

CIVIL RIGHTS STAR

When Rosa Parks was born, parts of the USA were segregated, which meant that black and white people did many everyday things apart from each other. There were separate schools, separate swimming pools, separate toilets and even separate water fountains. Rosa hated it. But surely not even she could have dreamt that her simple act of bravery would change *everything*...

NAME: *Rosa Louise McCauley Parks*

BORN: **4 February 1913**   DIED: **24 October 2005** (aged 92)

NATIONALITY: **American**

PROFESSION: **Civil rights activist**

After Rosa Parks' parents split up when she was just two, she grew up with her brother and mother on her grandparents' farm. They lived near Montgomery, the state capital of Alabama. It was a scary time for black people because of the resentment many white southerners felt towards them, blaming them for their own troubles. Thousands of African Americans were lynched, which meant that they were murdered – shot, hanged or both – by mobs of angry white people. Rosa heard of these happening. Meanwhile, she was bullied by white children, while her own grandfather once stood up to the Ku Klux Klan – a secret society of white supremacists.

At school, Rosa studied hard. Her mother was a teacher and education was very important to the family. But school wasn't the same for Rosa as it was for white children in Alabama. Their schools were well equipped, while schools for African-American children were very basic and lacked supplies. But even though Rosa had to leave school early to care for her grandmother and then her mother, she worked so that she could afford to go back and graduate from high school.

When Rosa was 19, she married Raymond Parks, who was a member of the National Association for the Advancement of Colored People (NAACP). Rosa became the first woman in Montgomery to join.

As well as in schools and swimming pools, at drinking fountains and public toilets, there were plenty of other ways in which black and white people were segregated. There was one more way that made Rosa very angry. Black people had to sit at the back of buses in seats labelled "for colored". The bus driver was also allowed to tell people where to sit. And when, on 1 December 1955, the driver asked Rosa to stand up so that a white man could sit in her seat, she said no. She was going to sit in that seat. And she was going to stay there.

The police were called, Rosa was arrested and she was fined $10 for breaking the law that allowed the driver to assign seats. She refused to pay, telling them that the fine was illegal. Others agreed. Together they decided to boycott Montgomery's buses.

What did they want?

An end to segregation on buses.

When did they want it?

NOW.

In fact, the peaceful mass protest took 381 days to achieve its aim. But at last the US Supreme Court ruled against Montgomery's segregation law. The protesters had won! Now, everyone could sit wherever they wanted. Even better, the civil rights movement kept going, leading to the Civil Rights Act of 1964. Discrimination was outlawed and now anyone could use any public facility. All because of Rosa.

She went on fighting for the rights of African Americans and was recognized with the Congressional Gold Medal and the Presidential Medal of Freedom. In 1999, *Time Magazine* named Rosa Parks as one of the twenty most powerful and influential figures of the twentieth century.

WHAT WOULD ROSA DO...?

Q *You've been left out of a WhatsApp group that every other girl in your class is part of. Why?! You just don't know and it's driving you mad. What would Rosa Parks do?*

A Rosa Parks didn't stand for discriminatory behaviour. She thought that all people should be treated the same. She would want to know why you weren't being included and she would tackle the problem head on. Rosa would contact the WhatsApp group admins and ask them to stop being unfair. The chances are, they'd back down immediately and add you to the group, but if they didn't, she'd protest. And she'd make herself heard.

> " I would like to be remembered as a person who wanted to be free... so other people would be also free. "
>
> ROSA PARKS

DR JANE GOODALL

CHAMPION OF CHIMPS

Jane Goodall is a primatologist, which means that she knows her chimps. She has spent over half a century patiently observing how they live and behave, and interact with each other. But she isn't just the world expert on chimpanzees – she works hard to protect them too. And even though she's now over 80, she still promotes the conservation of animals and the environment.

NAME: *Valerie Jane Morris-Goodall*

BORN: 3 April 1934

NATIONALITY: British

PROFESSION: Chimpanzee expert and conservationist

Jane Goodall's love of animals can be traced back to a toy chimpanzee called Jubilee that she was given on her first birthday. It was specially produced to celebrate the birth of the first chimp at London Zoo in 1935. She adored the toy chimp – and still has it – but no one could have guessed how hard she'd work and how far she'd go to look after real chimpanzees...

When she was young, Jane was fascinated by animal behaviour. Determined to watch an egg actually being laid, she once hid in a chicken coop *for five hours* to see it happen. (Meanwhile, her family called the police because they thought she was missing!)

But although there were plenty of chickens in the south of England where Jane grew up, exotic animals were in short supply. So she dreamt of faraway places instead... like Africa. Jane worked as a secretary and as a waitress to save the money to go. And her chance came in 1957, when a school friend invited her to Kenya.

In Nairobi, Jane met Louis Leakey – a British paleoanthropologist born in Kenya who was studying the origins of human life in Africa. He gave Jane a job as a chimpanzee researcher and she got stuck in at the Gombe Reserve in Tanzania. There, she witnessed a chimpanzee make a spoon from a twig, before dipping it into a termite nest to scoop up insects. It was a huge discovery. "At that time, it was thought that humans, and only humans, used and made tools... yet I had just watched a chimp tool-maker in action," she said, years later. It would change the way people looked at chimps *and* humans.

Sometimes, Jane's research methods were criticised – she gave chimps names rather than numbers, which some said made her view the animals less objectively. But after her 55-year study of chimpanzees in Tanzania, it's hard to argue with the fact that she discovered many new and amazing things about chimp behaviour – enough to make her the undisputed world expert.

In 1977, she set up the Jane Goodall Institute, which aims to encourage people to work together "to save the natural world we all share". The Institute says that "Dr Jane Goodall went into the forest to study the remarkable lives of chimpanzees – and she came out of the forest to save them."

In 1991, Jane founded Roots & Shoots, a youth-led community action programme. Its aim? To make the world a better place. Roots & Shoots began with just 12 students in Tanzania and has now grown to over 150,000 members in 130 countries.

The astonishing Jane Goodall has been showered with awards including the Kyoto Prize, the Benjamin Franklin Medal in Life Science, the Rainforest Alliance Champion Award, and the Primate Society of Great Britain Conservation Award. In 2002, she was named as a United Nations Messenger of Peace and the following year she became Dame Jane Goodall.

What a star.

WHAT MIGHT JANE DO...?

Q *You really, really, really want a pet. Cat, dog, rabbit, hamster, gerbil or fish, you're not fussy. (You quite like the sound of a bearded dragon, actually.) But your parents say no. What might Jane Goodall do?*

A This is a tricky one. Some parents just don't like the idea of a pet. Or they could be worried that you'll get bored and they'll end up looking after it. We don't know for sure what Jane Goodall would say, but she might suggest you volunteer at an animal sanctuary or a rescue centre for now. Then you can find out what it's really like to care for an animal for whenever you do own a pet.

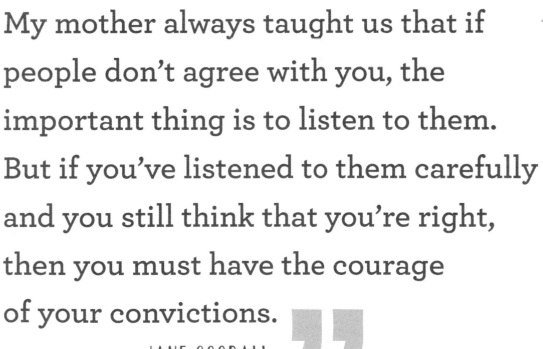

"My mother always taught us that if people don't agree with you, the important thing is to listen to them. But if you've listened to them carefully and you still think that you're right, then you must have the courage of your convictions."

JANE GOODALL

VALENTINA TERESHKOVA

ROCKET WOMAN

Human spaceflight is a pretty awesome thing. Since 1961, only a few hundred people have ever done it. Valentina Tereshkova became one of them and was the very first woman EVER to go to space. So how did a perfectly ordinary Russian do it? Easy. She had learned to do something fabulous. And it was this skill that got her noticed. The rest, as they say, is history.

NAME: *Valentina Vladimirovna Tereshkova*
BORN: 6 March 1937
NATIONALITY: Russian   PROFESSION: Cosmonaut

Valentina Tereshkova was born in a village in western Russia, the daughter of a tractor driver and a textile worker. Her father died in the Second World War when she was just two years old, so her mother brought up three children alone. Valentina left school at 16 to work in the same textile factory as her mother, but she carried on studying via a correspondence course. Meanwhile, she had quite possibly one of the coolest hobbies in the world – parachuting.

Fast forward to the 1950s, which is when the Space Race kicked off. It was a sort of unofficial competition between the USA and the USSR (Soviet Union). Each nation wanted to show that they were better at spaceflight, so each did their utmost to reach every space milestone first. The Russians stormed ahead by launching the first satellite – *Sputnik 1* – in 1957. Then they sent the first person into space in 1961. He was a man called Yuri Gagarin. Next, they decided to follow up this success by sending the first woman into space too.

Four hundred women were longlisted for the honour of being the first female cosmonaut. Remember the parachuting? This was a super handy way of getting back down to Earth after a spaceflight and Valentina already had a head start. So onto the longlist she went. Then she made it through to the shortlist and underwent cosmonaut training, which was tough with a capital T. It included surviving in a thermal chamber at temperatures of over 70°C and ten days in an isolation chamber. She went on weightless flights and did many, many parachute jumps. Finally, it was decided. She would be the one.

On 16 June 1963, 26-year-old Valentina Tereshkova rocketed through Earth's atmosphere on board *Vostok 6* to become the first woman in space. As she flew, she quoted Russian poet Vladimir Mayakovsky: *The sky! Take off your hat! I'm coming!* Then she orbited Earth 48 times and three days later parachuted the last 6km – gulp – back to Earth. Her mother was astonished. Valentina had told her that she was taking part in a skydiving competition.

So what did Valentina do next? Well, she graduated from the Military Air Academy with top marks and became the first woman to be a general in the Soviet Army. She headed the Soviet Committee for Women for 21 years. And she married a fellow cosmonaut and had the first baby whose parents had *both* been to space. In 2013, she spoke of her dream to take part in a mission to Mars. "I am ready," said Valentina Tereshkova, aged 76.

WHAT MIGHT VALENTINA DO...?

Q *Every single other person you meet knows what they're going to be when they grow up and you don't, and it's making you panic horribly. What if you still haven't found your perfect career by the time you're 18? What then?! What might Valentina Tereshkova do?*

A There is absolutely no way on Earth (or above it) that Valentina Tereshkova could have known that she was going to go to space when she was a kid, because space travel hadn't been invented. She did, however, know that she enjoyed parachuting, so that's what she did. We don't know exactly what Valentina would say, but she might simply suggest that you do what makes you truly happy.

"A bird cannot fly with one wing only. Human spaceflight cannot develop any further without the active participation of women."

VALENTINA TERESHKOVA

JUNKO TABEI

EXTREME MOUNTAINEER

Junko Tabei confounded many stereotypes to become a mountaineer. She was small – only 147cm tall. As a child, many thought that she was weak. And, most controversially of all, she was a woman. Fifty years ago, climbing wasn't something that women did. Junko was often told that she should be looking after children instead. But climbing was something that she loved and Junko was determined to do it, conquering mountains all over the world, including every continent's highest peak.

Junko Tabei

BORN: **22 September 1939**   DIED: **20 October 2016** (aged 77)

NATIONALITY: **Japanese**

PROFESSION: **Mountaineer**

• •

Junko climbed her first mountain on a school trip in 1949. This was an active volcano called Mount Nasu on the Japanese island of Honshū where she lived. Instantly, she was hooked. Here was an activity that wasn't a race. It was a challenge. (For the record, Mount Nasu isn't small. It measures 1,916.9m, which is nearly 50 per cent bigger than Ben Nevis, the tallest mountain in the UK. And Junko was ten years old. Wow.)

Unfortunately, mountaineering is an expensive sport and Junko's family simply couldn't afford for her to do it. So she gave up on the idea of being a mountaineer – for now – and trained to be a teacher instead. After university, she joined men's mountain-climbing clubs, but some criticised her, saying that all she was doing was looking for a husband. She wasn't, but she found one all the same on the slopes of Mount Tanigawa. From then on, her husband Masanobu Tabei – a well-known mountain climber – supported Junko's passion for climbing in any way he could.

In 1969, Junko founded a ladies' climbing club with the slogan: *Let's go on an overseas expedition by ourselves*. But again they were criticised. At that time in Japan, women were expected to stay at home while men worked.

When she tried to raise funds for an expedition to the Himalayas, Junko was told that she and her fellow mountaineers should be at home raising children. So Junko, who was working as an editor for a science journal, took on extra work to help pay for the trip. And in 1970 the women from the club tackled Annapurna III (7,555m) in Nepal. Four of them – including Junko – made it to the summit.

Next, the team decided to attempt Everest (8,848m). But only one team could tackle each route each season and they had to wait until 1975 to be able to go. After surviving an avalanche on the way up, Junko reached the tiny summit of Everest on 16 May 1975, becoming the first woman ever to climb the world's highest mountain. Boom.

It was while she was climbing that Junko became aware of the environmental impact of mountaineers. From then on, she campaigned for sustainable mountaineering, going on to study the subject as a postgraduate at university.

Junko went on to become the first woman to climb the tallest peak on each continent – collectively known as the Seven Summits. By the age of 69, she had climbed a breathtaking 160 mountains.

How awesome is that?

• •

WHAT WOULD JUNKO DO...?

 Your school is raising money for your favourite charity. It's to pay for something mega that will help a lot of people. But fundraising is getting harder and harder. Everyone else is running out of energy, even though you're so close to the end. What would Junko do?

 Just because others are flagging, doesn't mean you have to stop trying to raise money. Junko was a mountaineer, so she was used to uphill struggles. But she also knew how fabulous it was to get to the top of the mountain. Junko would tell you not to give up now. She'd tell you to keep going and she'd be proud of you for making it in the end!

 I can't understand why men make all this fuss about Everest – it's only a mountain.

JUNKO TABEI

WANGARI MUTA MAATHAI

MOTHER OF TREES

Wangari Muta Maathai is known as the Mother of Trees, but did you know that it's because she was responsible for the planting of 50 MILLION of them? It's an astonishing feat, but just one of the many great things that Wangari achieved during her lifetime. If she saw something wrong, she tried to fix it. And her efforts were recognised with one of the greatest honours of modern times – the Nobel Peace Prize.

BORN: 1 April 1940   DIED: 25 September 2011 (aged 71)
NATIONALITY: Kenyan
PROFESSION: Environmental and political activist

Wangari Muta was born in the village of Ihithe in the central highlands of Kenya in Africa. She started school when she was eight and was such a talented student that she moved to a Catholic boarding school in Nyeri three years later. After coming top of the class again, she went to high school. Then, in 1960, she got the chance to study in the USA, thanks to a programme begun by Senator John F Kennedy, before he became the US president.

Wangari returned to Kenya six years later with a degree and a master's degree in biological sciences. So then she must have stopped studying, right? Not exactly. Wangari worked as an assistant lecturer at the University College of Nairobi, got married, had a son and then became the first East African woman to be awarded a PhD – in Veterinary Anatomy – shortly before having a daughter.

Her academic career continued and Wangari became the first woman in Nairobi to reach senior positions at the university. Meanwhile, she campaigned – successfully – for equal benefits for women at the university. Aware that Kenya was suffering from deforestation, water and food shortages (leading to malnutrition) and that animals were dying out, she joined a number of organisations in an effort to address these issues. She also became the new chair of the Environment Liaison Centre, which meant that she was involved with the United Nations Environment Programme. More and more, Wangari began to realise that something had to be done about Kenya's environmental problems. Her answer was the Green Belt Movement, which she created in 1977. This encouraged Kenyan women to plant trees to fight against deforestation, generate income, prevent soil erosion and provide fuel. Since the movement began, more than 30,000 women have been trained in forestry and other vital roles that help them to earn a living while taking care of their environment. To date, a staggering 50 million trees have been planted, which inspired Wangari's nickname: Mother of Trees.

For years, Wangari tried to win a seat in Parliament, suffering arrests and beatings because of her opposition to the government. Finally, in 2002, she made it, with a jaw-dropping 98 per cent of the vote. By the following year, she was assistant minister for the Environment and Natural Resources.

In 2004, Wangari was awarded the Nobel Peace Prize "for her contribution to sustainable development, democracy and peace". She was the first African woman to do so. Oh, and she also found time to write four books: *The Green Belt Movement*; *Unbowed: a Memoir*; *The Challenge for Africa* and *Replenishing the Earth*. What a woman.

> " I don't really know why I care so much. I just have something inside me that tells me that there is a problem, and I have got to do something about it.

WANGARI MUTA MAATHAI

WHAT WOULD WANGARI DO...?

Q *You've fallen out with not one but two of your best friends and now they're acting as if you don't exist. You feel horribly left out. What would Wangari Muta Maathai do?*

A People often say that "two's company, three's a crowd", meaning that there's often disharmony when three friends are involved. Two might side together, leaving the third one out. It happens. But that doesn't mean you've got to live with it. Wangari was pretty good at getting people on her side. (She persuaded over 30,000 women to help protect the environment.) She would suggest that you speak to your two friends, perhaps one at a time. Try to sort out your differences. Once you make contact, it might be easier than you thought.

ZAHA HADID

STARCHITECT

Nicknamed the Queen of the Curve because of her dynamic designs, Zaha Hadid was responsible for some of the most imaginative buildings and structures ever. Skyscraper? Tick. Exhibition centre? Tick. Aquatics centre, art museum, opera house, bridge, ski jump, car factory and football stadium? Zaha designed the lot. She was strong-willed and daring, always striving for brilliance. Her fabulous designs dazzle the world today.

NAME: *Dame Zaha Mohammed Hadid*

BORN: 31 October 1950   DIED: 31 March 2016 (aged 65)
NATIONALITY: British and Iraqi
PROFESSION: Architect

Zaha Hadid was born in Baghdad, Iraq, where she was inspired by the work of famous architects Le Corbusier and Frank Lloyd Wright. (Look them up, go on.) After studying maths at the American University in Beirut, Lebanon, she went to London, where she studied at the prestigious Architectural Association School of Architecture. Here she was taught to let her imagination run wild. So she did, totally wowing her professors with her vision.

Now Zaha had to create a name for herself in a competitive world. It wasn't easy. She started out teaching at top universities around the world, including the Architectural Association, and Harvard and Cambridge Universities. In 1983, Zaha won a competition to design a resort complex in Hong Kong. Sadly, it was never built, since the client ran out of cash. Many other brilliant designs failed to materialise, but Zaha was not put off. She just kept on designing. It wasn't until 1993 that she was given the chance to see one of her designs in real life. This was the Vitra Fire Station in Germany – later turned into an exhibition space because it was an awkward shape for a fire engine.

Zaha's fame grew and she was given the opportunity to design more and more structures. She became known as "Queen of the Curve"

because of her fluid, fabulous and unbelievably imaginative designs. There's the London Aquatics Centre, built for the 2012 London Olympics, the Heydar Aliyev Museum in Baku, Azerbaijan and Galaxy SOHO in Beijing, China. Meanwhile, the Port Authority Building in Antwerp, Belgium looks like something out of a science fiction film. And then there's the Guangzhou Opera House in China, which Zaha said was inspired by "pebbles in a stream smoothed by erosion". Wow. Just wow. In fact, search for Zaha Hadid's designs online, sit back and prepare to be truly amazed.

In 2004, Zaha became the first woman to win the Pritzker Architecture Prize, something she described as "the Nobel Prize of architecture". In 2016, the year she died, Zaha also became the first woman to win the Royal Gold Medal award, presented by the Royal Institute of British Architects. But she never wanted to be recognised as a female architect or an Arab architect. Zaha was an architect, pure and simple. And just like her amazing designs, she was completely unique.

WHAT WOULD ZAHA DO...?

 Q *All the girls have started hanging around in the park after school. You think it's boring. You'd rather go to an after-school club and learn about something you're interested in, like art or basketball. But the girls are putting pressure on you to go. What would Zaha Hadid do?*

 A Zaha Hadid was one of a kind. She dared to be different. Just look at the fabulous buildings she designed. Zaha would tell you to do what feels right for you! She'd tell you to ignore the other girls and to have fun doing something way more interesting than getting a cold bottom on a swing.

" Women are always told, *You're not going to make it, it's too difficult, you can't do that, don't enter this competition, you'll never win it.* They need confidence in themselves and people around them to help them to get on. "

ZAHA HADID

MICHELLE OBAMA

GIRLS' CHAMPION

Michelle Obama was born in
Chicago, USA, where her childhood
was pretty ordinary. She grew up
living in an apartment. She went
to school down the road. She played
Monopoly. There wasn't a limo
or a world leader in sight...

Michelle LaVaughn Robinson Obama

BORN: 17 January 1964 **NATIONALITY:** American

PROFESSION: Lawyer, campaigner, once the First Lady of the USA

• •

Michelle's parents were determined that she and her older brother Craig would do well in life, and made them work hard for it. They were so good in school that both skipped a grade. Craig eventually won a place at Princeton – one of the USA's top universities. But when Michelle decided to go there too, her teachers tried to change her mind. She was just a girl. She was setting her sights too high, they said. But Michelle stuck to her guns and went to Princeton anyway, topping it off with a post-graduate degree at the world-famous Harvard Law School.

While working at a Chicago law firm Michelle mentored a young and charismatic lawyer named Barack. They fell in love, married in 1992 and had two daughters – Malia and Sasha. Michelle kept working and was invited for a job interview when her younger daughter was just a few months old. There was just one tiny problem: she didn't have a babysitter. But did Michelle let that stop her? Of course not. She took Sasha with her to the interview, nailed it and got the job.

And then Barack decided to run for president...

Michelle was lukewarm about the idea. She worried that politics would affect their family life. She was a private person and didn't want to be in the public eye. And she had her own career to think about. But the Obamas are a team and Michelle went for it, campaigning tirelessly for her husband. She had just one condition – to be away from home and their daughters just one night a week.

In 2008, Barack Obama won the Presidency. In 2012, he won again. For eight years Michelle was the First Lady of the United States. As well as her official duties, she worked hard on projects that she was passionate about. Perhaps her biggest success was the "Let Girls Learn" initiative, which she launched in 2015 to help the 62 million girls worldwide not in school. "I see myself in these girls," she said. "I see my daughters in these girls, and I simply cannot walk away from them."

She may no longer be at the White House, but one thing is for sure. Whatever Michelle Obama does next, she will own it.

• •

"When they go low, we go high."

MICHELLE OBAMA

WHAT MIGHT MICHELLE DO...?

 Q *You're really worried about the news. It's full of doom and gloom. Environmental disasters, wars, violence... It's never-ending! But what can you do about it? What might Michelle Obama do?*

 A Michelle Obama survived eight years of being in the media spotlight as the First Lady of the USA. She had first-hand experience of the news that you're worrying about. And look! She came out of it smiling. We can't be sure what Michelle would suggest, but she might tell you not to worry too much. She might also encourage you to speak up when and where you can about issues you're passionate about. Then you'll be doing your bit to change things.

90

JUDIT POLGÁR

GRANDMASTER

Chess might be an easy game to learn to play – it is! Try it! – but it's a fiendishly difficult game to master. It's also a game that is dominated by men. Garry Kasparov, one of the best players of all time, once said of Judit Polgár, *She has fantastic chess talent, but she is, after all, a woman... No woman can sustain a prolonged battle.* He was wrong, of course. And he changed his mind after Judit became the first woman ever to beat him in 2002.

NAME: *Judit Polgár*

BORN: 23 July 1976

NATIONALITY: Hungarian   PROFESSION: Chess player

Judit Polgár didn't become brilliant at chess by accident. Her father is László Polgár, a chess teacher and educational psychologist who once said that "geniuses are made, not born". But he didn't just say it. He decided to prove his theory too. His own daughters – Zsuzsa, Zsófia and Judit – became part of a very long research project that would eventually turn all three of them into chess champions.

László and his wife Klara home-schooled their daughters, focusing on languages and maths. The sisters were also taught to play chess – it was a field in which men and women could compete on equal terms. The Polgár sisters all became brilliant chess players, but Judit was the best of them all, first beating her father when she was just five years old.

By the time Judit was nine, she'd won her first international chess tournament. In 1988, when she was 12, Judit, her two sisters and Ildikó Mádl represented Hungary in the Chess Olympiad – an international competition organised by the World Chess Federation (FIDE). They won. Two years later, at the next Chess Olympiad, they did it again.

So, was there anything left for 14-year-old Judit to achieve? Oh, yes. In fact, she'd only just begun.

Judit – who was now one of the top 100 players in the world – entered competitions that were open to everyone. She wanted to compete with all of the best chess players, regardless of whether they were men or women. And in 1991, when she was just 15, she won the Hungarian National Championship! Except that wasn't all. Winning this championship meant that the FIDE declared her a Grandmaster, a title given to only the very best chess players in the world. Yet that *still* wasn't all. Judit Polgár became *the youngest person ever* to become a Grandmaster, beating the previous record-holder, Bobby Fischer.

Over the following years, Judit travelled the world to play chess. She won many tournaments and beat even more world champions along the way. At her peak in 2005, she was the 8th best player in the world. Meanwhile, she was the best female player in the world for an astonishing 26 years.

In 2012 she established the Judit Polgár Chess Foundation as a way of encouraging children to learn chess. And in 2014, she announced her retirement from competitive chess.

Judit Polgár has proved that she can play as well as men – and better than most. She is now the Head Coach of the Hungarian National Men's Chess Team.

WHAT MIGHT JUDIT DO...?

 It's so unfair. Everyone else goes to bed later than you, even children who are way younger! Why are your parents so strict? What might Judit Polgár do?

 Judit Polgár and her two sisters were home-schooled, which meant that their whole lives were completely different from that of most other girls. And that's just the way it is. Some parents say one thing. Other parents say another. Let's imagine what Judit might do in your situation; she might simply say to go with it. Your parents aren't mean. They're just doing what they think is right. (And, *psst*. If you get more sleep, you'll be brighter the next day. Honest.)

"It's not a matter of gender; it's a matter of being smart.

JUDIT POLGÁR"

MARTA VIEIRA DA SILVA

FOOTBALL SUPERSTAR

Marta Vieira da Silva – usually known as just Marta – is the most famous female footballer ever. She was FIFA Female World Player of the Year five times on the trot. She won both the Golden Ball *and* the Golden Boot at the FIFA Women's World Cup in 2007. And she's scored the most goals ever at FIFA Women's World Cup tournaments. But it's not been easy to get to where she is now...

NAME: *Marta Vieira da Silva*

BORN: 19 February 1986

NATIONALITY: Brazilian   PROFESSION: Football player

"It's a boys' sport," people told Marta, when she was young. "You have to play with a doll." She ignored them, of course, playing football barefoot on the streets of Brazil, where she was so talented that boys refused to join in. They were outraged that a girl could be better than them. Meanwhile, she played in boys' teams at school until she was banned – for being a girl.

Did that stop her? Of course not.

Marta's big break came when she was 14 and she was discovered by top Brazilian coach Helena Pacheco. She was whisked away to Rio de Janeiro, to train with one of the greatest football clubs in Brazil – Vasco da Gama. But after just two years, the programme ran out of cash and it was time to go... to the Brazilian town of Santa Cruz, where she played for two seasons.

So here's the thing. Men's football is a really big thing in Brazil. Women's football? Not so much. If Marta wanted to play at a top level, she was going to have to travel... 11,000km to be precise. Her new team was Umeå IK in Sweden. With Marta on their side, they won the 2003–2004 UEFA Women's Cup. In 2006, 2007, 2008, 2009 and 2010, Marta was FIFA Female World Player of the Year. Then it was back across the Atlantic to the USA, to play for Los Angeles Sol, FC Gold Pride and Western New York Flash. She was the top goal scorer every season. Meanwhile, Marta played for Brazil's national women's team in the FIFA Women's World Cup and in the Olympics too, often being the top goal scorer.

So what sort of a player *is* Marta? Quite simply, she's brilliant. She's got excellent balance. She's fast. She's got great ball control. She knows exactly what other players are going to do next. She's two-footed, which means that she can kick the ball well with both feet (not simply that she has two feet). She's committed too. And she's got terrific skills. Body swerve, nutmeg, step over, rabona – you name it, Marta can do it. (Just check out clips of her football skills online and prepare to be astounded.) It's no wonder that she wears the iconic number 10 shirt like all the best Brazilian players.

So if you ever feel like becoming a footballer, but are worried that the beautiful game is just for men, think again. Marta did.

She's now a United Nations Development Programme Goodwill Ambassador committed to empowering women.

WHAT MIGHT MARTA DO...?

Q *Everyone has the latest trainers. EVERYONE. The thing is, they're super expensive and your family can't afford them. Now you feel as if your friends are looking down their noses at you because you're not like the rest of them. What might Marta do?*

A Marta was the only girl in the boys' football team at school (until she was booted out because of silly rules) and the only girl to play football with boys in the street. Did she stop playing when they told her to go away? Nope. She wouldn't care what other people told her to do, whether it was about football or trainers for that matter. So Marta might tell you that just because everyone says you should do something, it doesn't mean that you have to do it.

"There's space for everybody. I play all the time with my male friends who are also professionals."

MARTA VIEIRA DA SILVA

EMMA WATSON

FABULOUS FEMINIST

Emma Watson starred in eight of the biggest box office smashes ever, before the age of 20. (And she didn't neglect her studies while she was doing it.) She's a fashion icon. She's a humanitarian. She's big on Twitter too, with over 20 million followers. She's also a feminist – and she doesn't think that's a dirty word. So that's why she's backing the idea that feminism isn't just for women. It's for men too. *Everyone* needs to get involved.

NAME: *Emma Charlotte Duerre Watson*

BORN: 15 April 1990

NATIONALITY: British

PROFESSION: Actor and UN ambassador

Emma was born in Paris and lived in the French capital until the age of 5. Then her parents split up and she moved to the UK. She had wanted to be an actor since she was very young and went to a theatre school to learn to act, sing and dance. She took part in school productions and won her first ever film role at the age of 9. It was a film that would shoot her to superstardom – *Harry Potter and the Philosopher's Stone* (2001). You may have heard of it. (Unless you're from Mars!)

Emma played the role of Hermione Granger for TEN YEARS, appearing in all eight Harry Potter films. But don't worry – she didn't miss out on school. She had five hours of lessons every day and proved that she was just as clever as Hermione by passing her GCSEs and A Levels with flying colours.

After filming on the last Harry Potter film wrapped, Emma went to university. Her English Literature degree took a little longer than usual because, in an epic example of multitasking, she was juggling her film career at the same time. (She filmed *The Perks of Being a Wallflower* in 2012 and *The Bling Ring* in 2013.) Oh, and because she loves fashion, she found time to be a model too. And win Best British Style at the 2014

British Fashion Awards (as well as a bunch of other awards).

So, she's a mega film star. TICK. She has a bucketload of qualifications. TICK. She's a great role model for girls. TICK. Surely that's enough for anyone?

Oh no.

Emma has also found time to promote girls' education in Bangladesh and Zambia. And in 2014, she was appointed as UN Women Global Goodwill Ambassador. Her tasks were to empower young women and promote gender equality via the UN Women's HeForShe campaign. In a personal, insightful and inspirational speech at the UN Headquarters in New York City, she launched the campaign. She told the audience that she was a feminist and that although she had been lucky enough to receive the same rights as men, not every woman had. There wasn't a single country in the world that had yet achieved gender equality. With the HeForShe campaign, she encouraged men to unite with women to fight together for equality.

Go, Emma!

WHAT MIGHT EMMA DO...?

 Q *You love social media. It's such a great way of staying in touch with your friends and letting them know where you are and what you're up to. But your dad has suddenly started getting really heavy. He's BANNED all forms of social media until you promise to keep a low profile. What might Emma Watson do?*

 A We don't know for sure what Emma would say but she might agree with your dad... Emma uses Twitter, Instagram and Facebook. But here's the deal. She doesn't go into details about her private life because she wants to keep it just that – private. And she wants to stay safe. So do yourself a favour and listen to your dad. He might have a point.

> **The saddest thing for a girl to do is dumb herself down for a guy.**
>
> EMMA WATSON

MALALA YOUSAFZAI

FEARLESS ACTIVIST

Malala Yousafzai is, quite simply, astounding. When the Taliban, an Islamic fundamentalist group in Pakistan, banned girls from going to school, she stood up to them. She criticised the Taliban on TV. She blogged about life under the Taliban's rule. She campaigned tirelessly for her right to an education. When the Taliban were angered by Malala's actions, she nearly paid the ultimate price for her bravery when gunmen tried to kill her. Did Malala let that stop her? No, she did not.

Malala Yousafzai

BORN: 12 July 1997

NATIONALITY: **Pakistani**

PROFESSION: **Education activist**

Malala Yousafzai was born in the Swat Valley in north-western Pakistan. She has loved to learn, ever since she was very young. Her father ran a school, somewhere she could satisfy her thirst for knowledge. But in 2007, everything changed. The Taliban – a hardline Islamic movement – took over the area where she lived and brought in new laws. One of these laws had a devastating effect on Malala: girls were banned from going to school.

To ten-year-old Malala, the ban was deeply unfair. "All I want is an education," she said. But what could she do? Plenty, it turned out. She spoke out against the Taliban on television. Then she began to blog for the BBC. She wrote about her fear of war, about living under the Taliban's rule and about her longing to go to school. At first, she blogged anonymously, but after her identity was revealed in 2009 she began to campaign in public. That year, the ban on girls' education was partially lifted! Soon afterwards, war broke out in Pakistan and Malala was forced to flee the Swat Valley. Once she was home again, months later, she carried on campaigning.

Malala's efforts were now becoming more and more well known and in 2011 she was awarded the International Children's Peace Prize and Pakistan's National Youth Peace Prize – the first of many, many honours. She was now receiving death threats, yet she went on speaking out for girls' right to education.

On 9 October 2012, Malala was shot and seriously wounded by Taliban gunmen. She was 15.

Offers to treat Malala poured in from all over the world. Eventually, she was flown to a hospital in Birmingham in the UK, which had a huge amount of experience in treating her type of bullet injury. And after an incredible recovery, Malala celebrated her sixteenth birthday on 12 July 2013 – now known as Malala Day – by giving a speech at the United Nations in New York City, USA. Meanwhile, millions signed a petition and Pakistan's National Assembly passed a bill that guaranteed free education for all children aged five to 16. The Malala Fund was set up the same year, to bring awareness to the need for girls' education and "to empower girls to raise their voices, to unlock their potential and to demand change."

In 2014, Malala became the youngest person ever to be awarded the Nobel Peace Prize in recognition of her struggle for the right of all children to an education.

She continues to make herself heard. "I don't want to be thought of as the girl who was shot by the Taliban, but the girl who fought for education," Malala says. "This is the cause to which I want to devote my life."

WHAT MIGHT MALALA DO...?

 You're being bullied and it's terrible. It's got so bad that you're afraid to say or do anything, in case the bullies find out and the bullying gets worse. What if they actually hurt you? What might Malala Yousafzai do?

 Malala suffered extreme bullying, but she didn't let it stop her from speaking her mind. We don't know exactly how she would react, but she might tell you to avoid situations where you're likely to meet the bully. But if that didn't work, then she might suggest that you stand up for yourself, even if it's scary. Act brave – the bully doesn't have to know that you don't feel brave. Tell the bully to leave you alone and then walk away. And make sure you tell a grown-up what's going on. They can help.

> So here I stand, one girl among many. I speak not for myself, but so those without a voice can be heard: those who have fought for their rights; their right to live in peace; their right to be treated with dignity; their right to equality of opportunity; their right to be educated.

MALALA YOUSAFZAI

WHICH ONE ARE YOU?

Answer these multiple-choice questions to find out which fabulous woman you are most like. Make a note of how many As, Bs, Cs, Ds or Es you score and then (and *ONLY* then) turn to page 110 for the big reveal.

 1 **What do you dream of being when you're older?**

a) A writer or an artist or a philosopher or... who knows? You haven't decided yet, but whatever you do, it'll be something wonderful.

b) Your future career is going to be something wildly creative, just like you!

c) A world leader, no question.

d) You're going to work in social services – you can't think of anything better to do than helping others.

e) You're going to be a politician. Then you can really make a difference!

 2 **The drama department at school has asked for volunteers to help paint the set. What do you do?**

a) You're way too shy to put yourself forward.

b) Everyone else, GET OUT OF THE WAY. This is the perfect job for you.

c) Painting the set? Er, no way. You'll be on the stage playing the lead role!

d) You'd be delighted to lend a helping hand.

e) The drama department can leave it up to you. You'll have a crowd of volunteers rustled up in no time.

 3 **Someone is being bullied in a WhatsApp group. Do you stand by and let it happen?**

a) Of course not. You add a pithy comment to the group and embarrass the bully so much that *they* leave the group.

b) No way! You go and tell a teacher, like, NOW.

c) You haven't got time for bullies. You contact the group admin and tell them to close down the WhatsApp group at once.

d) You comfort the person who's being bullied and promise to sort things out for them.

e) It actually hurts you that someone is being so mean. You get everyone together and confront the bully.

4 **It's the end-of-year disco at school. What are you going to wear?**

a) Something long and floaty and über laid back.

b) You simply can't decide between a flamboyant dress or a sharp suit. But whatever you choose, you're determined that people will notice you.

c) A crown.

d) Er, whatever you've got on.

e) Something practical, probably. You're not actually that bothered, tbh. You're far too busy organising the disco.

5 Your English homework is due in tomorrow morning, but you've been invited to the bowling alley after school. What do you do?

a) The English homework, of course. You can't wait to get stuck in.

b) You love to socialise, so clearly you're going bowling. But you also love to study, so you might stay up all night afterwards to do the homework too.

c) The homework. You're going to reach the top one day and studying is the way to do it. There's no time for fun!

d) You're going bowling. You love to be around other people.

e) Your head is telling you to do your homework, but your heart is telling you to go bowling. So you follow your heart, like you always do.

6 Your school has organised the best school trip EVER. There's just one problem – your best friend can't go because it's too expensive. What do you do?

a) It's not your style to follow the crowd, so you stay with your friend and keep her company.

b) This is a disaster! But you are so determined that your friend *will* go on the trip that you sell some of your belongings to pay for her.

c) You go on the school trip and don't worry about it. You're not responsible for everyone; you've got yourself to look after.

d) You plunder your savings account and lend the cash to your friend. She can pay it back whenever.

e) You go and see the head and ask them to find a way to reduce the price of the school trip. Once bungee jumping is off the agenda, it'll be much cheaper!

7 It's your worst nightmare. Your friends all want to try out the new climbing wall and you're terrified of heights. How do you get out of it?!

a) Er, what's the problem? You just tell them that you're scared of heights.

b) You tell everyone that you're going to visit the new art exhibition in town. It's way more interesting than dangling off a silly old wall, with far less chance of concussion.

c) You don't. You've overcome obstacles far scarier than a climbing wall to become the strong, powerful person you are today. You go for it.

d) If everyone else is brave enough to try it, you'll give it a whirl.

e) You take a deep breath and don't look down. You have faith that you can reach the top if you believe in yourself enough.

8 It's SO unfair. Every other girl in the class wears make-up, but your parents won't let you. What do you do?

a) Make-up is for the masses. You go and get a truly Bohemian henna tattoo instead.

b) Easy. You put the make-up in your bag and put it on once you've left the house. As long as you take it off again before you get home, your parents are never going to know.

c) You wear the make-up and deal with the fallout.

d) You can't bear to upset your parents, so you wait a year and ask them again.

e) You choose your battles wisely. Why wind up your parents over make-up when you'd far rather sign up for kick-boxing classes? You ask them if you can do those instead.

ANSWERS

Mostly a.

Give it up for
Virginia Woolf!
That's you, that is.
(See page 52.)

Mostly b.

You're a creative
powerhouse, like
Frida Kahlo.
(See page 60.)

Mostly c.

Catherine the Great
was unstoppable.
So are you!
(See page 28.)

Mostly d.

You and Harriet Tubman
are like peas in a pod.
There's nothing you enjoy
more than helping others.
(See page 40.)

Mostly e.

You follow your heart,
just like Joan of Arc.
(See page 20.)

TIMELINE

1646–1684
Elena Piscopia

1729–1796
Catherine
the Great

1815–1852
Ada Lovelace

1882–1941
Virginia Woolf

1897–1937
Amelia Earhart

1907–1954
Frida Kahlo

1940-2011
Wangari
Muta Maathai

1950-2016
Zaha Hadid

1964
Michelle Obama

110

69 BCE–30 BCE
Cleopatra

circa 43 CE
The Trung Sisters

973–1025
Murasaki Shikibu

1412–1431
Joan of Arc

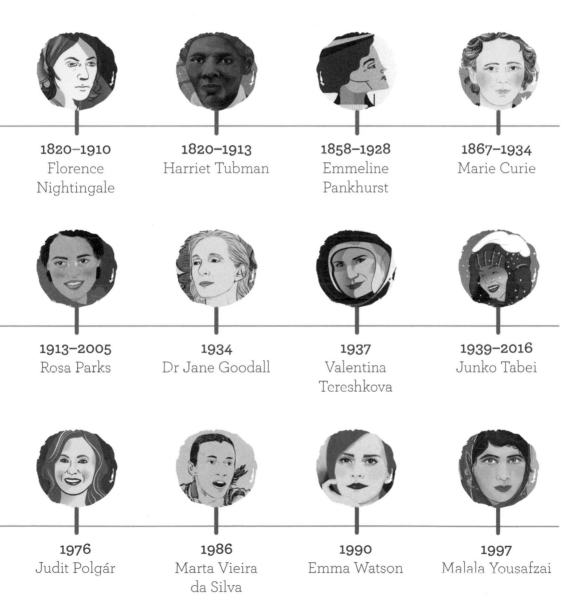

1820–1910
Florence
Nightingale

1820–1913
Harriet Tubman

1858–1928
Emmeline
Pankhurst

1867–1934
Marie Curie

1913–2005
Rosa Parks

1934
Dr Jane Goodall

1937
Valentina
Tereshkova

1939–2016
Junko Tabei

1976
Judit Polgár

1986
Marta Vieira
da Silva

1990
Emma Watson

1997
Malala Yousafzai

INDEX